AR Quiz
IL _____

BL _____

Pts. _____

D1455873

Demolition Derby Cars

By Jeff Savage

Consultant:
Todd Dubé, President
Demolition Events National Tour (DENT)

CAPSTONE
HIGH-INTEREST
BOOKS

an imprint of Capstone Press
Mankato, Minnesota

Capstone High-Interest Books are published by Capstone Press
151 Good Counsel Drive, P.O. Box 669, Mankato, Minnesota 56002
http://www.capstone-press.com

Library of Congress Cataloging-in-Publication Data
Savage, Jeff, 1961–
Demolition derby cars / by Jeff Savage.
    p. cm.—(Wild rides)
    Summary: Provides an overview of the history of demolition derbies and
describes the cars used and rules and highlights of these competitions.
    Includes bibliographical references (p. 31) and index.
    ISBN 0-7368-1516-3 (hardcover)
    1. Demolition derbies—Juvenile literature. [1. Demolition derbies.]
I. Title. II. Series.
GV1029.9.D45 S284 2003
796.7—dc21
                                                         2002012617

**Capstone Press thanks DENT Vice President Elizabeth Fitzsimmons for her
contributions in the production of this book.**

Editorial Credits
Matt Doeden, editor; Karen Risch, product planning editor; Kia Adams,
    series designer; Gene Bentdahl and Molly Nei, book designers;
    Jo Miller, photo researcher

Photo Credits
Capstone Press/Gene Bentdahl, 16, 17, 18
DENT/Craig Melvin, cover, 4, 6–7, 8, 10, 12, 14, 19, 20, 22, 25, 26, 28

1 2 3 4 5 6 08 07 06 05 04 03

Table of Contents

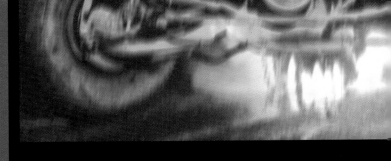

Learn about:

- Demolition derby events

- Drivers and prizes

- Common car models

CHAPTER 1

Demolition Derby Cars

Twenty drivers fasten their seatbelts. A loud rumbling noise fills the speedway as the drivers rev their engines. An announcer counts down from 10 to one and shouts "Go!" All 20 drivers steer toward one another. The demolition derby has begun.

The cars speed around the infield of the track. Their back tires kick up mud as they spin. The sound of crunching metal fills the air as the cars crash into each other. In minutes, all of the cars are smashed and covered in mud. Some cars take too much damage. Their engines stop and their drivers are out of the derby.

Soon, only a red station wagon and a white sedan remain. The station wagon backs into the sedan's front end. The sedan's engine stalls. The driver cannot restart it. The red station wagon is the last car to make a hit. Its driver has won the derby.

About Demolition Derbies

Demolition derbies are different from any other kind of motorsport. Drivers in other motorsports try to avoid crashes. Demolition

derby drivers run into their opponents on purpose.

Hundreds of demolition derbies are held each year at racetracks and county fairs throughout the United States and Canada. Anyone with a driver's license can compete in a demolition derby. Derby winners usually collect small cash prizes. They do not make much money, but the prize money is usually enough to pay for the cars they destroy.

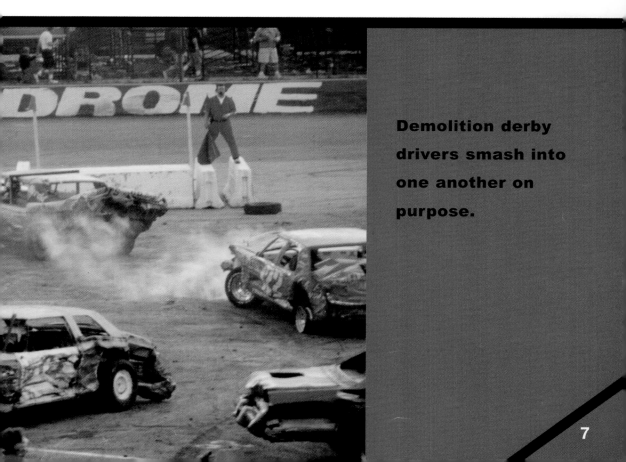

Demolition derby drivers smash into one another on purpose.

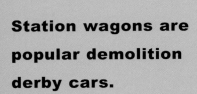

Station wagons are popular demolition derby cars.

Common Car Models

Most standard cars can compete in demolition derbies. Drivers can use station wagons, four-door sedans, and two-door cars.

Some oversized vehicles such as limousines are not allowed in derbies. Special demolition derbies are held for trucks, compact cars, and other types of vehicles. Large vehicles, including school buses and tractors, also have their own derbies.

Most demolition derbies are for cars. Drivers usually drive cars that were built in the 1970s. Common models include Chrysler Imperials and New Yorkers, Chevrolet Impalas and Caprices, Buick Electras, and Oldsmobile 98s.

Drivers use 1970s models for several reasons. Their strong steel frames can withstand a great deal of damage. The cars are also heavy. They usually weigh about 4,500 pounds (2,000 kilograms). Today's standard car models weigh about half of that total. Heavy cars can give more damage than lighter cars.

Learn about:

- **Early competitions**

- **Larry Mendelsohn**

- **The World's Richest Demolition Derby**

CHAPTER 2

Early Demolition Derbies

Car-smashing events became popular in the midwestern United States during the 1940s. Similar events were held in southern California around that time.

Early Demolition Derbies

No single person is credited with inventing demolition derbies. Several people were important in advancing the sport as it began. In 1947, Don Basile held one of the first modern demolition derbies at Carrell Speedway in Los Angeles, California. John Kaishian organized the first modern derby in the Midwest. His 10-car battle took place at Hales Corners Speedway in Franklin, Wisconsin.

One of the sport's most important promoters was Larry Mendelsohn. He organized a derby in 1957 at Islip Speedway in Long Island, New York. More than 4,000 fans attended the event. Mendelsohn began staging derbies regularly. Islip Speedway became

Demolition derbies have been popular for more than 50 years.

known as the top site for the derbies. During the 1960s and early 1970s, the ABC TV network broadcast many of these derbies. The broadcasts helped the sport's popularity grow.

The Greatest Derby Ever

The sport reached its highest point in 1973 at Los Angeles Memorial Coliseum. Father and son promoters J.C. and Cary Agajanian organized an event called "The World's Richest Demolition Derby." The winner's prize was $100,000.

This huge event included 100 drivers. Some of the most famous auto racers in the world drove in the derby. Among them were Parnelli Jones, Mario Andretti, and brothers Bobby and Al Unser. More than 50,000 people attended the derby. They saw Ken McCain win the event in his durable 1973 Ford LTD.

Learn about:

- **Body work**

- **Safety features**

- **Engine changes**

CHAPTER 3

Designing a Demolition Derby Car

Drivers often do all of the work on their derby cars. They start with a car that has a sturdy frame. They modify the car by making changes that will help the car perform well during the derby. They also add extra safety features. A beginner can make all of the necessary changes to a derby car for about $200.

Preparing the Derby Car

Demolition derby cars must be stripped of dangerous or unneeded parts. Drivers remove all of the car's glass, including the windshield, windows, and headlights. They also strip other items such as hubcaps and horns.

Next, drivers move some parts to the inside of the car. They empty and remove the car's fuel tank. They replace it with a smaller fuel tank that fits behind the driver's seat. Drivers also move the car's battery to the inside of the car. These sensitive parts are safer inside the car because they are less likely to be damaged there. Spilled fuel or battery acid can be dangerous to drivers and other people on the track.

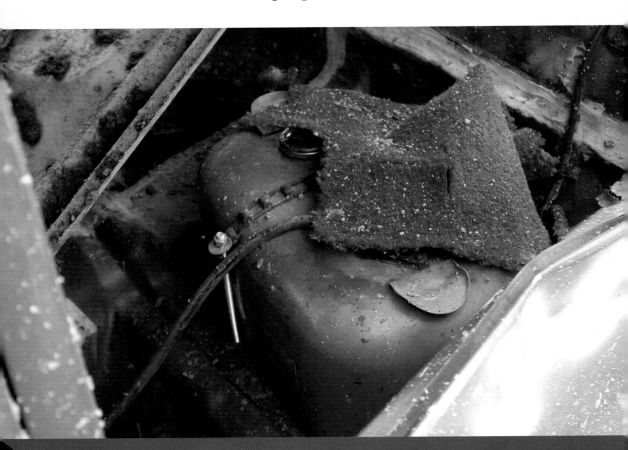

Drivers place a small fuel tank behind the driver's seat.

Drivers then tie down the trunk and the hood with chains. The doors must be either welded shut or tied shut with chains. These changes prevent parts of the car from coming loose during a derby.

Next, drivers strip the interior of the car. They remove all of the seats except the driver's seat. The carpeting, door panels, and dashboard instruments are also removed.

Holes cut into a car's hood allow officials to easily put out fires.

Safety Features

Safety modifications are the most important changes to a demolition derby car. A steel pipe called a roll bar usually is welded into the car to protect the driver. It goes across the driver's side door and over the driver's head. Foam padding is wrapped around the steering wheel.

Fire is one of the biggest safety issues in the sport. Drivers cut a hole about the size of a basketball into the hood. The hole allows track officials to easily put out fires that start in a car's engine. A fireproof metal wall stands between the engine and the driver. Each car also carries a fire extinguisher near the driver's seat. A crew of firefighters waits by the track at every derby.

Drivers also wear protective clothing. Strong helmets protect their head during crashes. Most drivers wear suits made of fireproof material. Some drivers even wear fireproof gloves and boots.

Derby officials and firefighters help protect drivers from car fires.

Demolition derby car engines often overheat. They sometimes catch fire.

Engines and Tires

Demolition derby cars have engines that are designed to stay cool as long as possible. The cars do not need powerful engines. Drivers sometimes replace a car's standard engine with a smaller one. A small engine produces less heat than a large one. The cooling system is the most important part of the engine. It is the target most other drivers try to hit. When the cooling system fails, the engine overheats and the car stops running.

The kind of tires a car has depends on each derby's rules. Many demolition derbies allow drivers to add mud and snow tires to improve traction on dirt and mud tracks. Other derbies limit the kinds of tires drivers can use.

Learn about:

- Events

- Rules

- Promoters

CHAPTER 4

Demolition Derby Cars in Competition

Usually, between 10 and 30 cars take part in each demolition derby. Some derbies have several events called heats. The winner or top finishers in each heat advance to the final event. The final derby is often called the feature.

Types of Derbies

Most demolition derbies take place on the muddy infield of a speedway or other racetrack. Cars must stay inside the track at all times. Most derbies are free-for-all events. Drivers do not work in teams.

Some events combine demolition derby with racing. Figure-8 races are an example of these events. Drivers in a figure-8 race go around a track in the shape of a number 8. The cars can crash into one another as they race to the finish line.

People have invented many other demolition derbies. In a backwards derby, drivers are only allowed to drive in reverse. In a balloon derby, cars have balloons attached to the front and the rear. A car is out of the competition when both of its balloons have popped.

Basic Rules

Demolition derbies are staged for fun. Drivers and fans do not want too many rules. But some rules are needed to keep the sport safe and exciting.

Most derby rules are for safety. Drivers cannot remove their seatbelts or helmets at any time. They cannot leave their cars unless the cars catch fire. Drivers also cannot crash into the driver's side door of another car.

Other rules help keep the action going. Drivers cannot leave the track and they must keep moving. Cars that stop moving are out of the derby. Cars also must be involved in at least one crash or aggressive hit every minute. Any driver who does not follow this rule is out of the derby.

A driver cannot leave a car unless the car catches fire.

The first National Championship Demolition Derby was held in the Pontiac Silverdome.

Promoters

A promoter is a group that organizes and runs an event. Most demolition derbies are sponsored by a local track. Drivers must pay an entry fee to compete in the derby. An average entry fee is $20. The promoter awards prize money to the drivers who win or finish high in the competition. A typical prize for first place is $500 to $1,000.

The Demolition Events National Tour (DENT) promotes derbies across the United States. In 1998, DENT promoted the first National Championship Demolition Derby at the Pontiac Silverdome in Michigan. The total prize money in this event was $20,000. Rick Harrington won the first-place prize of $10,000. Since then, this national event has been held at tracks in Ohio and Indiana.

Fans and drivers enjoy demolition derbies at all levels. It is one of few motorsports that is open to almost anyone.

Todd Dubé

Todd Dubé is the president of the Demolition Events National Tour (DENT). He started the organization in 1997 to bring the sport of demolition derby to a national level.

Dubé was born August 15, 1962, in Buffalo, New York. As a boy, he watched demolition derbies with his grandfather. At age 10, he began competing in other motorsports. He was especially skilled at motorcycle racing.

Dubé took part in his first demolition derby at age 20. He later won the 1996 Erie County Fair Demolition Derby and qualified for the New York State Championship.

In 1997, Dubé founded DENT. A year later, the organization promoted the first annual national derby competition. The winner received $10,000 in prize money, a gold ring, and the winner's trophy. The trophy is called the Franklin Root Award. "Franklin" is named after a speedway in Wisconsin. "Root" is named after Dubé's grandfather, Donald Root.

Words to Know

feature (FEE-chur)—the main event of a derby competition

figure-8 (FIG-yur ATE)—shaped like the number "8"

heat (HEET)—one of several early derbies that determine which drivers advance to the feature

modify (MOD-uh-fye)—to change; drivers modify the body and parts of a derby car to make it safer and stronger.

promoter (pruh-MOTE-uhr)—a person or organization that organizes an event such as a demolition derby

roll bar (ROHL BAR)—a steel pipe that is welded to a derby car to protect the driver

sedan (si-DAN)—a car with front and back seats and four doors

strip (STRIP)—to remove dangerous or unnecessary parts from a derby car

To Learn More

Huff, Richard M. *Demolition Derby.* Race Car Legends. Philadelphia: Chelsea House, 2000.

Savage, Jeff. *Demolition Derby.* Action Events. Berkeley Heights, N.J.: Enslow, 2000.

Savage, Jeff. *Demolition Derby.* MotorSports. Mankato, Minn.: Capstone Press, 1995.

Useful Addresses

Clear Channel Entertainment—Motorsports
495 North Commons Drive
Suite 200
Aurora, IL 60504

Demolition Events National Tour
P.O. Box 349
Lakeview, NY 14085

Internet Sites

Track down many sites about demolition derby cars.
Visit the FACT HOUND at *http://www.facthound.com*

IT IS EASY! IT IS FUN!

1) Go to *http://www.facthound.com*
2) Type in: 0736815163
3) Click on "FETCH IT" and FACT HOUND will find
   several links hand-picked by our editors.

Relax and let our pal FACT HOUND do the research for you!

Index